# Duck Dynasty:  88 Examples of Their Faith & Values

*by Sari Bryson*

## Introduction

While the Duck Dynasty Robertson family has a faithful following that surrounds their duck calls, they remain faithful in someone too: Jesus Christ.

It's been long known that Hollywood, and today's pop culture media doesn't readily acknowledge the Christian faith.

The Robertson's want to always encourage others to come to salvation in Jesus Christ, but reportedly the show's producers find this defining component of the Robertson's character to be a storyline that they shy away from. In fact, a great deal is misleadingly edited out.

"They pretty much cut out most of the spiritual things," Phil Robertson admits. "We say them, but they just don't run them on the show. Hollywood has run upon the kingdom of God, and there's a rub there. Well, we have to be as harmless as a dove and as shrewd as a snake in the way we deal with them."

The Robertson's who are active members of the White's Ferry Road Church of Christ have been known to bring others to Christ, and to evangelize everywhere they go.

This book will demonstrate how the Robertson clan believes in the Bible and Jesus, they have good old-fashioned values and they get along while having a great time.

Duck Dynasty is the #1 reality show and you will understand why that is so.

Duck Dynasty follows a Louisiana bayou family living the American dream as they operate a thriving duck call and decoy business while staying true to their family values – these values relate to the grace and salvation found in Jesus.

The show routinely includes scenes exhibiting time-honored American values, which, incidentally, certain current-minded television executives previously had a difficult time believing were marketable.

Some of the values that are seamlessly woven into many of the episodes include fervent faith, family loyalty, dedication to the work ethic, and valuing of our constitutional rights, Second Amendment rights in particular.

Duck Dynasty is unique among reality television in its unabashed depiction of faith. At the end of each show's episode, the family prays before breaking bread together. Phil is also often shown reading the Bible.

Phil Robertson fought against an early attempt by the show's producers to edit the word "Jesus" out of the family prayers. When the show's bosses tried to censor certain language in an effort to alter the image of the Robertson clan, he insisted that the editing cease.

During the next taping of the dinner scene, he prayed: "Father, thank you for the good food, thank you for our children, thank you for loving us and saving us. And I pray that you give these people that are filming us time to repent before you burn them for not using your name in a prayer." That ended the battle and brought Jesus' name back into the show.

Uncle Si used faith in addressing the gun control issue when he spoke to a crowd at the Texas Crawfish and Music Festival:

"Hey, look here, the president was just on the news about

gun control, but hey, luckily our congressmen and senators, they voted it down," Si said. "But look, America hasn't got a gun control problem, we have got a sin control problem. Nothing has changed with the human race, OK? We're a bunch of flawed people, OK? And 'Duck Dynasty,' look here, 'Duck Dynasty' is full of flawed people that have turned to Jesus, OK? That's the difference."

Kay spoke about how her marriage and family struggled for 10 years when Phil was leading a life filled with fighting and drinking. Kay was the first to be converted to Christianity – one year before her husband.

And even though Phil had kicked her and their three sons out of their family's home, she continued to stay in her marriage and pray for Phil's salvation. She and Phil have been married for almost 50 years. During their separation, Phil eventually turned his life over to the Lord. They attend the same church today where Kay received her salvation more than 38 years ago.

"My life was spiraling out of control in a hurry," Phil said. "It's literally what Jesus said, 'from darkness to light.'" After he became a Christian, Phil gave up drinking and "with a clear head" went back to Louisiana with his family and bought a house on the river. He then started working as a commercial fisherman while he built his duck call business from the ground up.

Si has said that he thinks everyone is in too much of a hurry.  He thinks one should take a sip of tea, mow a little grass and then if you get tired take a nap. "Work hard, nap hard, play hard.  When you get a break you gotta go to sleep fast."

When Si spoke at the local elementary school, he talked about Vietnam and said he thinks the kids need to know that someone paid a price for their freedom.  He told the kids there was a war in Vietnam that we were involved in, a lot of people died and there was a lot of blood.  He then said some of the kids may wake up at night with nightmares, but that may not be a bad thing.

And in his opinion, guns aren't the problem — "evil" people are. "I think it's the person behind it, and you know, who's doing these crazy, evil things. I just think it's evil and I think that certain people are evil, and whether they do it with a gun or a car or airplane or bottle of poison, you know, evil people are gonna do evil things whether they have a weapon or not

When Willie was asked about the renewed calls for gun control, "We're certainly pro-second amendment and pro-guns," he says. But it's not a business-driven stance. "It's not just our livelihood, but that's what we like to do, you know: we hunt."

"Faith is the number one thing in our lives, and so everything revolves around it: our marriages, our families, our business," Willie says unashamedly.

"That's how we can be so successful, that's how you can work with your family, that's how we can stay married, you know, because it's a higher calling than just that. If you stick with God's plan, it makes a lot of things a lot easier." "To put all the time and everything that it takes to make a show like this and have a bigger platform to get the message out and this particular vehicle of doing it, it's not a lot, but you know, it'll help us do the baby steps. ... In today's world of mainstream TV, it's a pretty positive view to actually show prayer and all that on TV. It used to be that was more common, and now you really stand out in the crowd."

"We're a brood that stays together and enjoys each other's company. I've seen enough train wrecks on TV, on these shows, It will be nice to see a family that sits down and has a meal together," Willie
said

Jase, Missy and kids before beard

The success of Duck Dynasty has shown that there is a large segment of America that appreciates the faith aspect of the show's brand of reality TV.

Jase says "The biggest question we get, you know people see us with our wives and they're like 'How did this happen?' 'Cause our wives are beautiful and we're not. It's amazing with all this social media, Facebook and Twitter, you hear people say 'Oh these women married these guys for their money,' because we're successful now, but what they don't realize is that when they met us, we didn't have any money.

We were all poor, and we've all been married for lots of years. I always think that's comical. We really came from humble beginnings. It's just been the American dream lived out, we do what we love to do, and it just worked out. But you know our wives are with us because of our spiritual qualities, which flies in the face of what most people think."

Si and Christine

When Jase was asked about the men's beards he responded "The beard also ties into our spiritual faith, that you shouldn't judge a book by its cover. I don't look at another human being and look at just their external appearance. Really I think if we looked at another person from the inside out we'd be a lot better off. I like people viewing me one way and then get around me and realize 'Man, was I way off.

Plus I think it keeps you grounded. There's a lot more to having a meaningful life than outward appearance or how much money you have or whether you're famous. I'm just not into those things. It's nice, the blessings of a successful business, but that's not our motivation whatsoever."

When Jase was asked what his biggest challenge he faced being part of Duck Dynasty he said "You know this is a platform to share our faith and try to show people that we believe there is a God and having a dynamic family life is important and can really bring you a lot of joy. We use it as a platform to make a difference in the world in a positive way.

That's probably my biggest challenge, balancing that with family life, of having the show, because kids by nature are immature. So having to sit down with my two teenage boys and say 'Look, just because 100 girls tweeted that you're the finest lookin' person on the earth does not mean that's true.' That has been a struggle.

You constantly have to tell them to have their own faith and be confident in who you are, not to let other people's opinion of you be the way you live your life. I think most people who get into the Hollywood world tend to live their lives based on what other people think, and that's a bad trap to get into. So we're trying to ground our kids and keep their heads in the right place. I credit our wives. They really are great women, spiritual women, who work harder to keep our kids grounded.

Korie's view on the secret to a good, lasting relationship: Laugh together, put your relationship first, and forgive freely.

When Missy Robertson was asked if Duck Dynasty has put pressure on her marriage she said, "We have a very strong marriage. There's not a whole lot that has gotten to us in our 22 years. I think it's because of the way we were raised and because of our faith. It's very rare that a couple like Phil and Kay would have four boys and all of them be married to their original wives for as many years as they have been.

And, of course, my parents have been married to only each other. So, when we got married, both Jase and I knew it was for life and for eternity. Of course, when you're getting married at 19 and 20, who can anticipate anything? Not that we haven't had challenges, but there's never been a question that we weren't going to be together for the rest of our lives.

People actually target him, thinking "he's going to be mine one day." But they don't know about our faith in God, and that is not an option for us. Truly, we are still highly in love with each other.  He still makes my heart skip a beat."

Miss Robertson - "One thing about the Robertson family — there is nothing that is taboo to talk about. I wasn't raised that way, but they definitely were. Everything is on the table. You have a problem, we're going to lay it out, and we're going talk about it. And nobody's going to bed until

it's ironed out. We have a lot of meetings in the late-night hours at our house because our children are our No. 1 priority. If we get famous and rich and lose our kids, it was for
nothing."

Willie and Korie with young children

Missy explains they go to church every week because a large part of their lives is involved in their church family. "That's not just something we say. It's not just a card that we punch on Sunday morning. We're very involved in each other's lives as brothers and sisters in Christ."

People want to come and see what's going on at the church where the Duck Dynasty family goes. The most likely want to know - why would "Duck Dynasty" people go to that church? Miss believes they're interested in that. "So, if there's any way that we can bring people to hear the Gospel of Jesus — because at White's Ferry Road you're going to hear the Gospel every Sunday — and if we can bring that to any visitors, we don't mind that at all. People are driving from all over the country to come to our church to see what's going on."

What would Missy want to say to her fellow Christians? "I want to say this for the Christian community. We get a little criticism from the Christian community because they feel like we're not saying enough on the show about Jesus, God and church. But we're not here to preach. We want to show Jesus."

"I hope the Christian community will understand that God is pushing this train, and we are not hiding that fact at all. We've got to make sure that we are approachable by the world, and I think that the men — all of their lives — have done a great job in that."

"Our show appeals to the world. Once we appeal to the world, we can attract them to Jesus, and that means being in the world, but not of the world, just like Jesus said. I hope folks will just be patient with us and really trust that God's using us in this way."

The entire Robertson family is active with the White's Ferry Road Church of Christ which meets just a few miles from the Duck Commander/Buck Commander warehouse in this northeast Louisiana town of 13,000.

Numerous shows portray families in non-traditional ways, distorting God's design. Each of these sitcoms brings a level of acceptance to culture. The Robertson clan gives a much-needed alternative. The traditional family does work. They are swimming against the current of culture in a sea of liberal media bias, but, miraculously enough, they are making it.

It turns out that the most important product Duck Commander markets isn't duck calls at all – it's family values rooted in faith.

The Robertson men spend time with their sons teaching them how to be men. They give them warnings of the dangers that await them in the world, but also encourage them to be distinct in their manhood.

The Robertson women teach the girls how to grow up and be women. It seems like it would be natural, but our culture hasn't seen this clear of a distinction between the genders since Home Improvement in the 1990's! Its ok for men to be men and for women to be women.

It's the Robertsons' authenticity that attracts viewers, media watchers say. But the Bible Belt particularly loves the Robertsons because evangelical Christians get messages from the show that other viewers might not. They see faith in Phil's interactions with his sons, in the boys' marriages and in the way they run Duck Commander, the business that made them millionaires.

Each episode ends with a speedy and unspecific prayer before a huge family dinner. The conclusion of each show is always the same; the family is together over a meal and Phil leads his family in prayer. It is not a silly prayer. It is a prayer thanking God for what He has done, in Jesus' name.

Phil, who has attended White's Ferry Road Church of Christ since age 28, previously said his family's humility despite their fame stems from their understanding that all blessings come from God and that everyone will die someday.

"Fame is rather fleeting, as you know, or should know," Phil Robertson told The Christian Post. "Money can come and go, and fame comes and goes. Peace of mind and a relationship with God is far more important, so this is the precedent that we've set in our lives. The bottom line is, we all die, so Jesus is the answer. Many have told me through the years: "I think I'll take my chances without Jesus." And I always come back and say, "so what chance is that?"

People enjoy reality television for many reasons, including the shock factor. Television producers know that reality often needs to be altered to make interesting viewing or overemphasize certain stereotypes.

That might explain some of the tension the Robertsons seemingly feel with the producers of 'Duck Dynasty.' People are especially interested in Duck Dynasty because the Robertsons' family and friends are outrageous and unpredictable characters. Yet they also are relatable and likable. They are God-fearing, family-oriented people who enjoy life.

In the first two episodes, the producers bleeped out words said by Willie and Korie to make it appear that they cursed. The family complained. As Al Robertson explained, "We don't cuss."

Since the cast of Duck Dynasty doesn't swear in the show or otherwise, families can gather around the tv knowing there won't be any "surprises."  There are very few family shows anymore on television that don't have sexual innuendoes, but Duck Dynasty is one of them.

It's been long known that Hollywood and today's pop culture media doesn't readily acknowledge the Christian faith. The Robertson's want to always encourage others to come to salvation in Jesus Christ.

The Robertsons provide good clean fun in a secular world. Their innocent humor is precisely what today's television often lacks.  They have been known to bring others to Christ, and to evangelize everywhere they go.

"Despite the spiritual material cut out of the show, we're so blessed for what we can get in there. That's really unknown in today's TV on a regular, big TV network like that." – Miss Kay

The clan with clean-shaven Alan

Even before "Duck Dynasty" Phil Robertson developed a wide following for his powerful, revivalist-style gospel preaching. He talks about ducks. He shares Jesus.

As the show has gained popularity, though, crowds once in the hundreds have swelled into the thousands. Phil Robertson said he and his sons Al and Jase preach the same message of faith, repentance and baptism wherever they're invited. "We don't have godly people and followers of Jesus owning the channel that we're on or filming what we do," Phil said. "So what you see on TV is a functional, godly family, but there's not a whole lot of Gospel and Bible verses."

"However, the audience can be reached in other ways than the TV show," he added. "We're going to be making a Robertson family tour. You'll see the real family when you get us in some arena somewhere and it's just us telling people the good news of Jesus."

Phil explained how the preaching all started before the tv show, Duck Dynasty: He was down in New Orleans at the Superdome and he gave a duck call demonstration and said, 'Folks, I'm not an ordained minister but I think I'm going to preach you a little sermon. My message is to get human beings to love God, love their neighbor and for the life of me I just don't see the downside of human beings not being so mean to one another and actually care for one another and not steal from one another and not murder each other for their tennis shoes. That's the message I have."

Phil believes that people do bad things in this world because there is a love problem. "A loving person is not going to pick up a spear or a knife because when the Ten Commandments were written it was before guns, and God was saying, 'Look, quit murdering each other.' Now I'm just trying to say, 'Folks let's try to love one another no matter what the color of their skin.'

Phil and Miss Kay had a code with their kids growing up. Phil told them that he'd give them three licks if they disrespected their mother, if they were fist fighting with each other, or if they ever tore up perfectly good equipment for no good reason. He and Miss Kay made sure the kids were loved and were taught how to love their neighbor.

We had very few rules and regulations. I would say, 'If you want to stay up all night, that's your prerogative. Getting up in the morning and catching the school bus.' We didn't go in there and say, 'Time to get up.' We taught them to be responsible.

When it came to teachers I told them, 'You're going to have great teachers, fair teachers and some are going to be poor but always remember they are your teacher. Shut up and sit down and obey them and get out with a fair grade and onto the next one.' I backed the teachers no matter what.

Phil has said he's not going to run for political office. In all his speeches he seldom gets political. Most of his messages are far more common sense and spiritual. He doesn't use any of the terminology like left wing and right wing. He uses language like godly and holiness.

The Robertsons are able to stay true to themselves. There is an element in these guys from their raising by Phil and Kay — they are so self-confident. They are not arrogant. They don't care what anybody else thinks.

Jase does not care what anyone else thinks about the decisions that he makes. And I think that is a huge element in the show, because so many people want to please the masses in these sitcoms and reality shows. They want the ratings — what should I say to get good ratings?

"We are going to be true to ourselves first. We didn't know if the show was going to work. We sat around in a meeting with the Benelli company years ago and said, "Wait a minute — reality shows? They live on conflict, dysfunction and trying to get a rise out of each other, for the cameras. We are Christian people. We try to do the opposite. So, we don't see how this is going to work." – Missy Robertson

When Missy was asked during an interview what the goal was of Duck Dynasty she replied– "This has not been our goal in life — to have a TV show and to be rich and famous. I never saw that happening. I said I don't mean to be a prophet. I felt some things, but I never saw this happening. Now that it's happened, we realize — and we realized when it was happening — this is something that God is doing for us and is doing through us. This is not because of us."

"I feel a very weighty responsibility in this — sometimes overwhelming — where I feel like, I hope that we're doing our father in heaven justice with this show. Because I want to make sure that, through the things God has given us, we can glorify him, we can lead people to him, we can show the sacrifice that he made with his son and how appreciative we are of that fact. That's the most important thing to us. And if it gets to where we've lost that perspective, please Lord, take this away, because we do not want this for us. We want it for Him. So far, I truly feel like that we are doing some good for Him. And we do hear that quite often."

"The success of the show has shown that there is a large segment of America that appreciates the faith aspect of "Ducky Dynasty's" brand of reality TV. "I mean if nobody watches it then who cares? Still, that's not to say that each episode is modern-day "Andy Griffith Show," Willie Robertson says and continues:

"I mean, dad [Phil] is pretty crude and some of the stuff he says, I'm like 'holy cow.' Still, I heard the same speech when I was 15. He's just like that, I mean, he just lays it out there the way it is. And I think a lot of guys see that in their dads too: just kind of a little bit different attitude, different generation. And he's certainly open with it and lays it out there."

Willie, when asked about sexual banter between Phil and Kay – which is regularly featured –how it makes him feel, Willie takes an approach that might surprise some. "I'm going to take a different spin and say it actually makes me feel proud," he explains. "I'm glad that they still do, and that they're happily married. I'm proud that they are, you know, I'm glad that they're so open with themselves. Hopefully I will be too at that age."

Duck Dynasty works because it brings Christianity into an everyday cultural experience.

Even though the guys on Duck Dynasty have a very bizarre life, the show does try to represent these characters as simple, real life people.  Christianity doesn't become the spectacle of the show, it simply becomes an element of authenticity. And that certainly appeals to those who are Christians.

At one point during a drinking binge, Phil told Kay to take their children and leave. She did, but eventually Phil came back.  Phil then just went 100 percent for the Lord and started reading his Bible every day.  He wanted to teach and preach, and really wanted to turn his life around so it was very impactful for his children to see that type of change.

Phil was baptized and became a Christian. He left a life of drinking, carousing and fighting. Phil said "I looked at my life and I said, 'Man, I am lucky to be alive! What in the world good did I ever get out of all that?"

Robertson and his wife, Kay, have been winning souls for quite a while. For two decades, until his public speaking began taking them out of town so often, they hosted a house church and conducted weekly Bible studies.

For the Robertson's four sons — Alan, Jase, Willie and Jephtha — going to bed at night with people still in their home studying Scripture was normal. "I would get up for school, and there would be two to three people asleep on the couch, their wet clothes over a chair," Alan said. "At some point Dad had baptized them in the river near our house."

Friends and relatives estimate that the Duck Commander has baptized more than 300 in the nearby Ouachita River. His first public-speaking opportunity came in the early 1990s when fans asked him to give a duck-calling seminar at the Superdome in New Orleans.

Afterward, the crowd applauded enthusiastically. Invitations to speak poured in. Within a year Kay became his scheduler, travel agent and traveling companion.

"Now, when we go places, the planners tell us they know Phil is coming to save the unsaved, and they really work to get people there who don't know Jesus," Kay Robertson said.

Booked nearly two years in advance by churches and organizations, he draws crowds and standing ovations nearly everywhere he speaks.  Tall and in his 60s, Robertson begins by talking about duck-hunting tactics and demonstrating his duck calls.

Next, he lays down a kind of hunter's Bill of Rights straight from Noah's story in the Bible — emphasizing God's permission for mankind to kill and eat animals after the flood. He concludes with his personal testimony — sharing what Jesus has done for him and can do for them.

"I liken it to the book of Acts," he said. "I just give them the simple gospel — Jesus was born, died, was raised and is coming back. Then I'm on down the road."  Regardless of where he speaks, he preaches the simple gospel.

"That will take care of any false doctrine," he said. "If they're saved, they might not have everything straight. I doubt if we do. But if they hear the gospel and obey it, I'm happy for them."

Phil Robertson quotes scripture and Thomas Jefferson frequently to defend his family's stances on Christianity, guns and hunting. He spoke on how God and Thomas Jefferson gave him the right to speak freely and did not forbid the killing of animals. "The only foundation for a useful education in a republic is to be laid in religion. Thomas Jefferson said that."

"The Founding Fathers would be shocked that there was not biblical instruction in our schools," Phil said earlier this year at a conference.

Phil Robertson carries a Bible in his bag everywhere he goes. He believes we all have a God-given right to live free.

When Willie was asked about the renewed calls for gun control, "We're certainly pro-second amendment and pro-guns," he says. But it's not a business-driven stance. "It's not just our livelihood, but that's what we like to do, you know: we hunt." And in his opinion, guns aren't the problem — "evil" people are.

Jase is very involved with his kid's lives. Every day he tries to teach his kids something positive.

John Luke is very quiet on the show, but he says he's actually very talkative. He says he's quiet around his grandpa out of respect for him.

Willie and his wife adopted their son (who is bi-racial) when he was a baby. Their decision to adopt was heavily influenced by a friend/minister who had also adopted a bi-racial child at the time. Willie and Korie's biological children are John Luke, Sadie and Bella. They are also raising Rebecca as a foster child, who was formerly an exchange student. Now they're raising her as their daughter.

In Korie's Twitter bio she calls herself the "proud wife" of Willie, and touches on their unique family situation. "Mom to four awesome kids plus a sweet exchange student who became ours. Love my big family. Thankful. God is good."

When Missy was asked during an interview what fame has the show "Duck Dynasty" presented to the marriage, she responded, "We have a very strong marriage. There's not a whole lot that has gotten to us in our 22 years. I think it's because of the way we were raised and because of our faith."

Miss Kay isn't the only "Miss" of the family. Everyone calls the women of the show by their first names, and adds "Miss" at the beginning. It's the proper Southern thing to do.

Kay's favorite family tradition is on Wednesday nights she picks up the grandkids to take them to church. Along the way they do something fun like go to the library, eating out or going to the park.

When Korie was asked during an interview what the best and worst part was about working with kin, she responded, "The Robertson family laughs a lot so we always have fun. Willie and I don't always agree, but we share a bed so we can't stay mad forever."

Jessica Robertson gets along with everyone in the family equally because she admits she doesn't like confrontation.

When Jase isn't working on the family business or hunting, he loves spending time with his wife and doing sports with the kids.

Phil's favorite thing to do when he's not working on family business is to stand in front of a crowd of people with a Bible in hand for about 45 minutes.

When Willie was asked which family member would be elected President, he said himself: "You can ask the rest of the family and they would agree. I like politics and I know how to solve problems. Shake hands, kiss babies and make promises. No problem. I'm Willie Robertson and I approve this message."

When someone described the likability of Duck Dynasty - "I think people are especially interested in 'Duck Dynasty' because the Robertson family and friends are outrageous, unpredictable characters. Yet they also are relatable and likable. They are God-fearing, family-oriented people who enjoy life."

All of the members of the Robertson family, as well as series regulars John Godwin and Justin Martin, are active members of the White's Ferry Road Church of Christ. Phil and his oldest son Al (who hasn't appeared on the show as of yet) serve as church elders.

Uncle Si says he always travels with three things: a gallon jug of iced tea, his plastic cup, and his Bible. (He probably also takes his wife. Although the show often gives the impression Si is single, he's married to Christine. They too are active members of the White's Ferry Road church.)

Willie says when the family gets together to watch Duck Dynasty, they all laugh their heads off. "If I'm not in a scene, then I don't know what they did, so I laugh just like everyone else does. And you never know how it's going to come out after editing. We'll make comments about that day, or the day we filmed it, and how hard it was."

A&E asked the Robertson's to wear different bandanas on the set so that the producers could tell the brothers apart. Willie chose one that looks like the American flag and rarely wears it in public.

Although Si's wife is never mentioned and has never been on the show, he and his wife Christine have been married for 43 years.

Al, the only Robertson not on the show yet, was a pastor for 20 years at White's Ferry Church of Christ. He and his wife Lisa have two girls, Anna and Lisa.

Rumors that Phil Robertson threatened to quit the show if guns and God are removed are not true. According to the Facebook page of radio station 93.1 The Wolf, TV network A&E asked Robertson if they could remove the religious- and firearm-related content from the show — but Robertson answered 'no.'

"If we can't pray to God on the show, we will not do the show," he reportedly said. "God and guns are a part of our everyday lives to remove either of them from the show is unacceptable.

Si is a Vietnam veteran.

America is hungry for entertainment that represents family values. We live, we work, we go to church, we play, we pray. There's nothing uncomfortable to explain to the kids who might be in the room. For television standards of 2013, "Duck Dynasty" is one of the cleanest shows you can watch — and the Robertson clan includes someone who appeals to virtually every age group.

Despite the spiritual material cut out of the show, Miss Kay says, "We're so blessed for what we can get in there. That's really unknown in today's TV on a regular, big TV network like that."

"To put all the time and everything that it takes to make a show like this and have a bigger platform to get the message out and this particular vehicle of doing it, it's not a lot, but you know, it'll help us do the baby steps. ... In today's world of mainstream TV, it's a pretty positive view to actually show prayer and all that on TV.  It used to be that was more common, and now you really stand out in the crowd." – Willie

## Summary

The Duck Dynasty cast knows all too well the challenges of trying to work with Hollywood, while not compromising any of their moral values. Hollywood certainly doesn't make it easy, and sadly this doesn't look to be changing anytime soon.

However, this camo covered group is the perfect example of a Bible-reading, gun slinging, family loving group of people and it is their genuine character that is making Duck Dynasty such a hit.
They provide good clean fun in a secular world. Their innocent humor is precisely what today's television often lacks.

Kudos to the Duck Dynasty cast for being who they are, and standing up for what they believe! That America.....is most definitely courage at its finest!

Made in the USA
San Bernardino, CA
28 July 2014